FINAL
TESTIMONIES

FINAL TESTIMONIES

BY
KARL BARTH

edited by **Eberhard Busch**
translated by **Geoffrey W. Bromiley**

Wipf & Stock
PUBLISHERS
Eugene, Oregon

This book is a translation from the German edition of Karl
Barth, *Letzte Zeugnisse,* published by Theologischer Verlag,
Zürich. It appears by permission of Theologischer Verlag.

Wipf and Stock Publishers
199 West 8th Avenue, Suite 3
Eugene, Oregon 97401

Final Testimonies
By Barth, Karl
Copyright©1977 Theologischer Verlag Zurich
ISBN: 1-59244-402-4
Publication date 10/21/2003
Previously published by Wm. B. Eerdmans Publishing Co., 1977

CONTENTS

TRANSLATOR'S PREFACE   7
FOREWORD   9

TESTIMONY TO JESUS CHRIST   11

MUSIC FOR A GUEST —
A RADIO BROADCAST   17

LIBERAL THEOLOGY —
AN INTERVIEW   31

RADIO SERMONS CATHOLIC
AND EVANGELICAL   41

STARTING OUT, TURNING ROUND,
CONFESSING   51

EPILOGUE   61

TRANSLATOR'S PREFACE

Particular weight and solemnity has always been attached to last words. It is for this reason rather than for any outstanding merit or originality that Karl Barth's final testimonies to the gospel command our interest. What were the things on his mind when life was obviously drawing to a close? What did he most want to say or stress within the confines of his specific assignments? Where is the essential core of his thinking and message?

Perhaps the first of the chosen pieces brings us closest to the heart of the matter. When asked to testify to what Christ means to him, Barth answers clearly and boldly but refuses to be pressed into a purely individualistic or private statement. Christ means to him what he means to all others. Even in the most personal confession he thus preserves the sense of community, not just in the sense of "for me and for all others too," but in the sense of "for all others and for me too."

The other statements express no less typical Barthian themes. Love of Mozart goes hand in hand with a first and last conviction that theological work serves the preaching and pastoral ministry. Authentic liberalism is to be espoused and not opposed, and church matters, including theology, are for all Christians, not for clergy as distinct from laity. The Roman and Reformed churches can grow together ecumenically as the former develops the ministry of the word and the latter the complementary ministry of the sacrament. The pattern of church life must be one of ongoing moving forward which is also a moving back, of constant exodus and conversion, in which the abiding factor is confession of the one Lord Jesus Christ.

The old humor is there, the element of surprise, a little more reminiscing, as one expects in the old, and the kindly spirit which gradually replaced the early pugnacity. The words are simple, and they add little to what Barth has said in his previous writings. But behind them stands a wealth of thought and experience endowing them with a peculiar poignancy and force.

It is fitting — perhaps even symbolic — that the last of these final pieces breaks off in the middle of a sentence. Barth had always recognized that theology can never achieve a final utterance. His masterpiece, the *Church Dogmatics*, remained a magnificent but uncompleted fragment. The last word, after all, cannot be spoken by us. It has to be spoken to us by him who speaks the last word as well as the first.

The words of Karl Barth are ended, but the Word of God which he attempted to serve lives and endures forever.

Pasadena   G. W. Bromiley

FOREWORD

The Karl Barth Society of North America was founded October 1972 to promote "a critical and constructive theology in continuity with the work of Karl Barth." Among its various activities, the Society is committed to encouraging and, where possible, assisting the publication of Barth's posthumous works. Accordingly I am grateful to be able to congratulate the Wm. B. Eerdmans Publishing Company for making Barth's *Final Testimonies* available to English readers.

It is fitting that the translation of this little book, whose importance far exceeds its brevity, should come from the hand of Geoffrey F. Bromiley. He, far more than anyone else, has been responsible for the translation of the thirteen monumental volumes of the *Church Dogmatics*. Beginning with Volume I, 2, he shared the editorship with Professor T. F. Torrance. He was the sole translator of the last five volumes, and he translated large portions of three of the preceding volumes. The church of Jesus Christ and the English-speaking world are immeasurably indebted to the tireless and unselfish labors of Professor Bromiley.

As for Barth's *Final Testimonies*, we can only echo the felicitous sentiments expressed by the translator in his preface.

Arthur C. Cochrane
President,
The Karl Barth Society of North America

TESTIMONY TO JESUS CHRIST

I HAVE BEEN ASKED TO REPLY IN A KIND OF TESTIMONY to the question what Jesus Christ is for me. The request jolted me at first, for I felt reminded painfully of the earlier question of Pietists and the present-day question of theological existentialists. Nevertheless, this does not alter the fact that in its own way and its own place this, too, is a serious question. I will try to answer it with the necessary brevity.

How can I do so, of course, without saying at once and consistently, in a way that determines and controls everything from A to Z, that Jesus Christ is for me precisely — no more, no less, and no other than — what he was, is, and will be, always and everywhere, for the church which he has called together and commissioned in all its forms, and for the whole world according to the message which he has entrusted to the church? If I were to single out something special that he is for me, I should be missing what in fact he is specifically for me. He is for me in particular precisely what before me, outside me, and alongside me, he is for all Christians and indeed for the whole world and for all men. He is this specifically for me too.

Jesus Christ is the basis of the covenant, the fellowship, the unbreakable relationship between God and man. I, too, am a man. Hence he is the basis of this covenant for me too.

Jesus Christ in the uniqueness of his existence has

made himself known to Christians as the free gift of this covenant proffered to all men. I, too, may be a Christian. Hence he is obviously for me, too, the demonstration of God's grace at work in this covenant — the grace which is free in relation to me but which also frees me.

Jesus Christ in his life and death has borne and borne away the sin of the world and the church. I, too, belong to the world which has been reconciled to God. I, too, am a member of the church which is called together by him. Hence I, too, may live and die in the light of the righteousness and holiness of God which defies all the faults of the world and the church.

Jesus Christ has done his work in the form of the history of his reconciling life and death which took place on behalf of the world and the church. Since I, too, belong to the world and am a member of the church, the history of my life as a man and a Christian may become the history of my own justification and my own sanctification by God in spite of all opposition.

Jesus Christ as the first to rise from the dead is the promise that the victory of his life and death will one day be generally and definitively manifested in him. As I may believe in the victory that he has already won, living and dying in this faith I may hope for this coming manifestation as the manifestation also of my justification and sanctification accomplished in him.

Jesus Christ is the Word of God spoken to all. As I, too, am one of the all, and as I too, believing and hoping in his promise, may see myself as one who is addressed by his Word, I am empowered, commissioned, and liberated with heart and hand and voice to bear witness to him as this Word of the love of God. As he has made himself responsible for me before God, I, too, am destined for an active response to the Word of God which is directed to all.

This is what Jesus Christ is for me — for me too.

Music for a Guest —A Radio Broadcast

*I*NTERVIEWER. IN A LETTER OF THANKS TO MOZART[1] we read: "What I thank you for is simply this, that whenever I hear you I find myself set on the threshold of a good and orderly world both in rain and sunshine and by day and night, and as a twentieth-century man I find myself gifted each time with courage (not pride), with tempo (not exaggerated tempo), with purity (not tedious purity), and with peace (not indolent peace). With your musical dialectic in his ear a man can be young and grow old, can work and rest, can be content and sad, in short, can live."

Karl Barth wrote this letter to Mozart on Mozart's 200th birthday in 1956. It need not surprise us, then, that our guest today, Professor Karl Barth, has asked that only Mozart's music be heard on our broadcast. To begin with we shall hear the fourth movement, the allegro, from the little G-minor symphony [K. 183], and no one will find it odd that we are beginning this broadcast with music even though Professor Barth is not a musician but a theologian.

Professor Barth, you have written an article "An Appreciation of Mozart"[2] in which you refer to him somewhere as "this one and no other." In your address on "The Freedom of Mozart"[3] you even quote a saying

1 Karl Barth, *Wolfgang Amadeus Mozart*, Evangelischer Verlag, Zollikon, 1956.
2. Sunday edition of the N.Z.Z., February 13, 1955.
3. At the commemoration on January 29, 1956.

of his father in which he calls Mozart a prodigy. Now I want to ask you what Mozart really means to you as a non-musician, as a theologian.

Barth. Before answering I want to put a question to you, Frau Schmalenbach. How is it that you are putting this particular question to me? As you have pointed out, I have written about Mozart. But that was a very little book. I have also written, as you know, a whole row of bulky volumes on what are apparently very different subjects. I have also said and done many things besides, some of them in the area of politics. How is it that you are interested in me in the specific field denoted by your question?

I. There are various reasons for this, Professor. As our guest you are one of the subjects of our broadcast but the other subject is music. And I think that if anything is known about you by people who are not theologians and not versed in theology, it is that Mozart is for you the epitome of all things musical. (Happily Mozart is the most requested composer in my program.) Again, although you have written *Romans* and the Barmen Declaration and the massive *Church Dogmatics,* and many other books that I know nothing about, you have also written the little work on Mozart. So you have something specific to say on this subject too.

B. Well, I am pleased to hear what you have just said, that I am not the only one to ask for Mozart, that it is not just a fad of mine, but, as I said in the book, there are many good folk who have found what I think I find in Mozart and who thus put in requests for him. Now what is it that we find? I might put it this way. What I hear in Mozart is a final word about life insofar as this can be spoken by man. Perhaps it is no accident that a musician spoke this word. But I hear a final word which holds up, as I stated in the extract you read, a final word which lasts, a final word to which one can always return and with which one can always begin afresh. For ultimately we must all begin afresh each day — and I make this new beginning best when I listen to Mozart. Right!

I. You also wrote, Professor, that Mozart meets the very human need for play.

B. Yes, I was very serious when I said that. But I think that in the last resort one can understand what play is only when one also knows what work is. My own life has been filled with a good deal of work. And it is only in relation to work that I have been able to see what it was in Mozart that rested on work but was in effect play.

I. You do not see Mozart, then, as a facile, outmoded, or even rococo composer?

B. Not at all. What we hear in him is play against a background of work, pleasure against a background of life — of life even in its suffering and the bearing of personal and other troubles, of which Mozart had plenty.

I. A whole heap . . .

B. Yes indeed. For me it works out this way. I could not understand Mozart as I do if I myself in another way did not know something about the seriousness of life. I am not speaking now of the pressures of writing the *Dogmatics* and preaching and so on. I am thinking of the place from which I drew and heard and received all this. From this place I have heard a harmony which Mozart obviously heard first before he composed it, and for me this has always agreed with what I have heard from a very different place than he did.

I. From a very different place, Professor?

B. From a very different place . . . yes, for now you are asking me as a theologian.

I. In the Bible? In the Word of God?

B. Yes.

I. We shall have to talk about theological matters too. But first another Mozart request.

B. Good. Let's have something playful this time, for example, the third movement, the allegretto, from the *Quintet in E Major*.

I. That's K.452. We shall be hearing Vladimir Ashkenazy and the London Wind Soloists.

The question of play in serious life has led us to the allegretto. Play is pursued in a wholly dedicated way by children. My question, then, is what place music had in your childhood. What was your relation to it then? Did you yourself play any music?

B. I tried, but it didn't turn out so well. So I became a listener. My father was musical and played the piano well. As I recall — I mention it in my little book — it is impossible for me ever to forget — I was four or five at the time — how he played "I amino mine" ("Oh, happy fate!") from *The Magic Flute*. This affected me — I can't say how — and I remarked: He's the one!

I. So you were not even a schoolboy at the time. Where was this, Professor?

B. In Berne.

I. Did you spend all your schooldays in Berne?

B. Yes, from the first grades to the highest. Then I began my university work in Berne and from there went to Germany. A highlight in Berlin was a semester I took with Harnack.

I. Did you go on to do a doctorate with him?

B. No, I went back to Berne for a semester.

I. Did you sing student songs?

B. Yes, I could manage that — a whole semester. But I didn't work much. I had been a real worker in Berlin but I passed my days with student cheerfulness in Berne.

I. But that is also important in the sense of play.

B. Yes, it was perhaps the one time in my life I had to enjoy life. And I did so — very radically.

I. When you became a pastor, had you already done your doctorate?

B. No, I never did a doctorate at all. I . . .

I. So that is why you are listed only as an honorary doctor?

B. That's *all* I am.

I. "All" in inverted commas! But is this possible?

B. It's the way it was. I was not aiming at an academic career. I wanted to be a pastor. I was this for twelve years, first in Geneva, then in Safenwil. That was all I knew.

I. And why did you not remain a pastor?

B. In my work as a pastor I gradually turned back to the Bible and began my commentary on Romans. This was not meant as a dissertation. It was written for its own sake. I thought what I had found in Romans might interest others too. Then I received a call to Göttingen and became a professor. My whole theology, you see, is fundamentally a theology for pastors. It grew out of my own situation when I had to teach and preach and counsel a little. And I found that what I had learned at the university was of little help in this. So I had to make a fresh start and I tried to do this.

I. Did you not miss as a professor the daily round of the pastor's life?

23

B. No, I cannot say that. I just did the same thing on another level, the academic level, teaching, talking with students, and so on. This was not a real break for me.

I. I suspect, Professor, that you have always done your work, as pastor or professor, with the same joyousness that one can continually catch in Mozart?

B. Yes, although naturally with the necessary changes and transpositions in view of the different circumstances. But I have always enjoyed my work. And if we are now to hear another piece of Mozart's, I should like something in A major, which has always been a basic key in my own life. So perhaps we might turn again to the young Mozart and I suggest the andante, that is, the second movement, from the *Symphony in A Major.*

I. We shall be playing, then, from the little A major, K. 201, as recorded by Bruno Walter and the Columbia Symphony Orchestra.

From the young Mozart we now go back to the young Barth and his commentary on Romans, which hit with the force of a bomb. How great its effect really was came out at the beginning of the Hitler era when you issued declarations which became authoritative for a great part of the church.

B. Yes, but the church conflict was much more closely related to my life and theological work. The theology in which I decisively tried to draw on the Bible was never a private matter for me, remote from the world and man. Its theme is God for the world, God for man, heaven for earth. This meant that all my theology always had a strong political side, explicit or implicit. You have mentioned my book on Romans. It came out in 1919 at the end of the first world war and it had a political effect even though there is not much about politics in it. Already in Safenwil I was deeply involved with my congregation, a working-class one, and I came up against the social question there. I had to wrestle with industrial problems and became notorious as "the red parson of Safenwil." So political involvement was not something that came later. When I arrived in Germany I had so much academic spadework to do that at first I was rather restrained in this foreign country. But then came Hitlerism. I plunged into politics again, and there emerged the Barmen Declaration, to which you referred. Now this does not contain a single direct word about politics but it certainly was a political factor, perhaps due to my influence in the shaping of the document, and it was seen thus by friend and foe alike. Note that all this was part of a context for me. Later, when I came to Basel, I did not become active in politics again. I had never really been, although I had been a member of the Social Democratic Party in Safenwil. I did not want to get involved in this way again in Basel.

I. In party politics?

B. But my political position was plain enough. In the Mozart year, 1956, the uprising took place in Hungary, and I became notorious throughout Switzerland because I would not join in condemning the communists. The reason was not anything I said but the fact that I did not say anything. I did not join the chorus of accusers that came forward then. My interest in politics continues to the present day.

I. The present day — do you find Czechoslovakia a repetition of 1956, or a parallel to it?

B. Things are quite different there. There is no recurrence in history.

I. Have you said anything about Czechoslovakia?

B. I have not had to, because the necessary things have been said by others who know the political situation much better than I do and can speak on the subject much better than I can. I have been very pleased at the reaction in Switzerland, especially in the church. Many excellent things have been said. I have nothing to add, and could not have said them better.

I. With all the problems that trouble us, for example, when we read the morning paper, do you think there is hope we might learn something?

B. Certainly. Nothing is in vain. I cannot look without hope, then, on a world where small steps can be taken with the prospect that one day everything, literally everything, will be made new. When we view the whole we can view the parts too without despair or agitation. And even here, if a little out of season, we can thus experience some joy. We might now go back to Mozart, and in sharp contrast to present reality, and to what concerns me day by day as I take part in the political life of this world, I suggest that we listen to something jolly from Mozart, a little song which is almost frivolous — almost so — but which I like to hear from time to time because of its refrain: "Silence — I will say no more." Yes indeed, I will say no more . . . we also need to be able not to think that we always have something to say. Let us listen then.

I. Irmgard Seefried is the singer accompanied by Erik Werba.

Mozart's little song is a kind of pause between two serious discussions. We shall now turn to the hopeful ecumenical sphere which engages people today and in which you have played some part. You were even in

Rome and saw the Roman church reaching out to ecu-menicity. Surely you have a good deal to say about this.

B. Yes, but you must understand that my own con-tribution in this sphere was only a modest one. I was in Amsterdam in 1948 when the World Council of Churches was established. I even gave the first address there on the theme "The Confusion of the World and God's Plan of Salvation." The line I took was that the theme ought to be reversed. We should deal with God's plan first and then with the world's confusion.

I. Typical of Karl Barth?

B. To be sure. But after that I did not have time to devote to the ecumenical movement. I had other things to do. But then the Vatican Council came and showed me how in a private way, with no commission from anyone, I might engage in a little ecumenical move-ment of my own. A very little one! This is why I went to Rome, visited Paul VI, and engaged in discussions with the Jesuits and Dominicans. It was all very stimu-lating and worthwhile. On occasion I have done a few other things too. Here on the Bruderholz we have good relations between the Reformed and Roman Catholic communions. And so I do a little here and there.

I. On the Bruderholz where your home is and so in your own neighborhood?

B. Yes. I tread the boundary here with my physician and friend. He is a Roman Catholic and a good doctor who has kept me alive . . .

I. You have been very ill, and we are glad to have you with us today. Now, Professor, do you think we could say that what is happening in the Roman Catholic Church is a reformation?

B. That is too strong a word.

I. A reforming?

B. Well, one might say a renewal. But that comes to the same thing. What is happening in the Roman Catholic Church is a late flare-up of the 16th-century Reformation. Perhaps that is saying a little too much, but one might possibly say there is a connection. At any rate I get along very well with many Roman Catholic theologians, often much better than with our Protestant ones . . .

I. Now for the other side of my question. Is there not a certain danger that our confession, which reformed itself or made its protestation in the 16th century, has in the meantime become ossified and is not making headway?

B. Yes, it has become ossified. It is resting on its laurels, and that is the big danger. But I must also say that when I hear Reformed and Roman Catholic sermons one after the other on the radio I am pleased to find some agreement. Even without a visible ecumenical movement the church is on the march. I am no optimist. We will not experience reunion. But it's a great deal that we are now talking to one another. And even when we talk alongside one another, there's a certain harmony.

I. Harmony. A musical term. What about some more harmony from Mozart?

B. I think we should have something from the secular side of Mozart. What about the ending to *The Abduction from the Seraglio:* "I shall proclaim your noble highness"?

I. Where good and evil harmonize . . .

B. Yes indeed.

I. We shall hear Erika Köth, Lottle Schädle, Fritz Wunderlich, Friedrich Lenz and Kurt Böhm, with the chorus and orchestra of the Bavarian State Opera,

Munich, conducted by Eugen Jochum.

This finale from the *The Abduction* is almost the finale of the present broadcast. I want to bring into our last round of discussion a term which is very important in your theology. When in our enthusiasm for Mozart we stammer rather than speak, we often speak of him today as a charismatic musician or of his music as charismatic. But *charis*, or grace, is a central word in your theology, and it needs some explaining.

B. I am glad you said we are *almost* at the end. To turn then to your question. You wanted to hear something about my life and thought. I will say this. So far we have spoken a little about theology, about the world and politics, and briefly about the situation in the church. But mark this, Frau Schmalenbach, I am not ultimately at home in theology, in the political world, or even in the church. These are all preparatory matters. They are serious but preparatory. We have to learn to stand in them, to do so fully, and I want to do this quite cheerfully, but we have also to learn to look beyond them. This brings us to the word you mentioned, the word "grace." Grace is one of those terms that is rather overworked today. I myself have used it a good deal and have to use it. But "charismatic"? Why, one can have a charismatic chess player or football player! It's like the word "miracle." So care is needed.

I. But when we are speaking to a theologian, to Karl Barth, another grace is meant . . .

B. . . . Another grace is meant. And this brings me to where I am really at home, or, should I say, to him with whom I am at home. Grace itself is only a provisional word. The last word that I have to say as a theologian or politician is not a concept like grace but a name: Jesus Christ. He is grace and he is the ultimate one beyond world and church and even theology. We cannot lay hold of him. But we have to do with him. And my own concern in my long life has been increasingly to emphasize this name and to say: "In him." There is no salvation but in this name. In him is grace. In him is the spur to work, warfare, and fellowship. In him is all that I have attempted in my life in weakness and folly. It is there in him. I suggest then that we finish with Mozart as a sacred composer. I myself have always been very fond of the little *Missa Brevis in D Major*, again by the young Mozart. It comes from much the same period as the symphony we heard earlier and is K. 194. I suggest that we play the conclusion: *Agnus dei, qui tollis peccata mundi, miserere nobis, dona nobis pacem:* "O Lamb of God, that takest away the sins of the world, have mercy upon us, grant us thy peace." This is what we shall now hear.

LIBERAL THEOLOGY
—AN INTERVIEW

INTERVIEWER. DR. BARTH, WHEN I ASKED YOU TO TAKE part in this broadcast, "What does it mean to be liberal?", you described yourself in the questionnaire as a "liberal." But so far as I know, as a theological layman, you are everywhere regarded as the one who overthrew Protestant liberalism. Is there not some contradiction here? Or do you call yourself a liberal only in the political sense?

Barth. When you invited me to this interview, I took it that you wanted to know whether and in what sense I would see myself as an opponent of liberal theology — we will not go into the question whether, as you say, I overthrew it! But when I found that I was supposed to declare and confess myself to be, as it were, a "non-liberal," I felt prodded or urged to surprise you with the statement that I, too, am a "liberal." I had primarily in mind the situation in theology in which I have the reputation of not being a liberal. I wanted to jolt and shatter this myth a little. So I said that I, too, am a liberal — and perhaps more of a liberal than those who call themselves liberals in this area. I was not for one moment thinking of the political world. But if you want to know, I am not unprepared to state my position there too.

I. You would not wish, then, to be stamped as "neo-orthodox"?

B. When I hear this term I can only laugh. For what does orthodox mean? And what does neo-orthodox mean? I am acquainted with what is called orthodoxy. In theology it is usually equated with the theology of the 16th and 17th centuries. I respect this. But I am far from being of this school. On the other hand, I am accused of being orthodox because I have found much help in it. Others have usually not even read the older orthodox. I myself was so liberal that I read them and found many good things in them. But "neo-orthodox"! I just find it comical when people use terms like that.

I. You have just said: "I myself was so liberal that I read the older orthodox." Are you using the word "liberal," then, in the sense of unprejudiced or open — not wearing blinkers — and in contrast to being dogmatic?

B. Let me begin by saying that when I call myself liberal what I primarily understand by the term is an attitude of responsibility. For freedom is always a responsible thing. And that means further that I have always to be open — here we come, do we not, to what is usually meant by freedom? I might then add a third element. Being truly liberal means thinking and speaking in responsibility and openness on all sides, backwards and forwards, toward both past and future, and with what I might call a total personal modesty. To be modest is not to be skeptical; it is to see what one thinks and says also has limits. This does not hinder me from saying very definitely what I think I see and know. But I can do this only with the awareness that there have been and are other people before and alongside me, and that others still will come after me. This awareness gives me inner peace, so that I do not think I always have to be right even though I do say definitely what I say and think. Knowing that a limit is set for me too, I can move cheerfully within it as a free man. Does that make sense?

I. I think so. If I may put it in my lay language . . .

B. You have now used a word I don't like to hear. You are making an old but false distinction between lay people and what? The hierarchy, theologians, a priesthood? No such distinction exists. I, too, am a layman. A layman is simply one who belongs to the people. All of us can only belong to the people — I mean, of course, God's people, which is all-embracing. In this people of God we are alongside one another. One has studied theology and another has not, but the one who has studied theology, and still does so, is not for this reason better than the other, the so-called layman, or different from him. You are not even to say to me: I am no expert in this matter, as though to say: It doesn't concern me. It concerns you just as much as it does me. Is that clear too?

I. Yes indeed. Thanks. We are recording this in your study, Professor, and on your shelves I see your life's work, a dogmatics in many volumes. Now a word like dogmatics or dogma or dogmatic is close to implying a belief in revelation. But both dogma and belief in revelation are usually felt to be the antithesis of such concepts as liberal, free, and relative. You have just relativized your own work a little, if one may say so. Is there not a contradiction here ?

B. Quite the opposite! I will begin with the concept of revelation, which is perhaps more important than that of dogmatics. Revelation means that one who was hidden has shown himself. One who was silent has spoken. And one who had not so far heard has perceived something of this. Revelation does not mean that a stone tablet has fallen from heaven with truth

35

written on it. Instead, it is a history between that one and us. I myself do not see what this has to do with lack of freedom or illiberalism. On the contrary, in my long life I have found that in listening to revelation I have become free in the sense described earlier. And for this reason I regard myself both before and after as a free man.

I have indeed become so free as to be able to write dogmatics — which many notable theologians are afraid of doing. Most theologians, especially today, write only little pamphlets and articles and Festschrift contributions. I was never content with this. I said to myself: If I am a theologian, I must try to work out broadly what I think I have perceived as God's revelation. What I think *I* have perceived. Yet not I as an individual but I as a member of the Christian church. This is why I call my book *Church Dogmatics*. Church here does not mean that the church is responsible for all that I say but that I as one member of the church have reflected on what may be perceived in revelation and tried to present it to the best of my conscience and understanding. I do not see, then, how the concept of dogma or dogmatics either can or should have anything whatever to do with illiberalism.

I. Revelation, then, is not a fixed code which we have to keep to once and for all but an appeal to people to understand?

B. Yes, and above all it is a history. God has acted, acts, and will act among men. And when this is perceptible, it is his revelation. To have a relation to this revelation means, then, to enter into this history of God's action, looking to past, present, and future (so far as one can), and asking what one has to think about it and say about it.

I. And human freedom — what place has that in revelation?

B. Revelation itself is the gift and work of freedom. Its origin is the freedom of God. God is free in his grace in turning to us men. When I accept that, I can react to it only as a free man. Hence the antithesis, freedom or revelation, is a false one. I do not become a slave but free when I hear the revelation of this free God. "If the Son shall make you free, you shall be free indeed," we read in John's Gospel. I have tried to hold to this. Perhaps I have not heard well enough. Perhaps I have not in fact been free enough. But it is along these lines that I have lived.

I. What does man become free from?

B. Perhaps above all else from himself — so that he does not regard himself as so terribly important. And free also from certain ideas and ideologies. The world is full of principles and rigid opinions of all kinds.

I. Is liberalism one of the ideologies?

B. Yes, once it becomes an "ism." One should be on guard against all words ending in "ism." Liberalism, too, might become an ideology — a rigid thing — and then it's no longer worth anything. In this sense, precisely as a liberal, I am free from liberalism. But the decisive point is to be free from oneself and not to regard oneself as the center of the world and the source of all truth, but to keep at a certain distance from oneself and to be able to move at this distance, not putting on protective armor.

I. You have told us to be on guard against all "isms." This brings us to another sphere that we have touched on, that of politics. You, Professor, have been heavily engaged in politics in your life. Was this out of a sense of responsibility as a citizen or because of your theological concerns?

B. I will simply say that because of my life as a Christian and a theologian, first as parson and then as professor, I have naturally lived in the *polis* too. As a theologian one does not float like a little angel above the earth. Questions are constantly put to one which are to be called political questions. As pastor in a village in the Aargau — more than fifty years ago now — I was so liberal that in contrast to the liberals of the day I could become a Social Democrat and earned the title of "the red parson of Safenwil" — though that didn't worry me much.

I. I might remind our younger listeners that that would be a much more radical step before the first world war than it is now.

B. Certainly. There would be nothing very remarkable about it nowadays. But at that time it was a bad thing to be a Social Democrat. It was tantamount to being a Bolshevik, at least in the Aargau.

I. And not only there!

B. But it didn't matter to me. Later I went to Germany, to Göttingen, and there, just after the German defeat in the first world war, I found myself in the company of professors who all swore by the German flag, the Kaiser, Bismarck, and so on. The only thing for me to do was again to take the side of the left — for what I found in Göttingen did not smack of freedom.

I. We again have an illiberal "ism," that of nationalism.

B. Of course! In Germany, too, I at first joined the Social Democrats. But I was not very active. I had to work long hours in my study. I had better things to do than take part in German politics. But I still identified myself with the left. I became a Social Democrat out of pure liberalism, don't you see? Only when 1933 came did it become obvious to me where I had to stand and where I had not to stand.

I. It is well known that in 1935 you lost your chair at Bonn because of your opposition to Hitlerism. Why was this opposition to National Socialism once again opposition to an "ism"?

B. In the last resort simply because I saw that the good German people had begun to worship a false god! It was a sorry and almost impossible thing, was it not, that a fellow like Hitler should suddenly spring up. They put his picture all over the place — even on altars — and they did it intellectually too . . .

I. Yes, some of the statements of German theologians were prize ones . . .

B. Or not such prize ones! In short, I acted instinctively at this point. I did not need to consider whether I should oppose all this. In a limited circle of German Evangelical churches I did my best to put up some resistance to this development.

I. To return to your socialism, if you will pardon another word ending in "ism." It is not to be supposed that you were a Marxist?

B. No, I was never that, decidedly not. I was never a doctrinaire socialist. What interested me about socialism in Safenwil was especially the union movement. I studied this for some time and helped it too, so that when I left Safenwil there were three flourishing unions where there had been none before. This was my modest involvement in the labor question and my very limited and for the most part practical interest in socialism. Naturally I did other things too. But the doctrinaire or ideological aspects were always marginal for me.

I. A possibly small but practical act of helping to improve the lot of little people in the teeth of the strong — an act of freedom?

B. Yes, that was my concern in those days. But that is long ago. Such things are taken for granted nowadays, are they not?

I. Socialism and liberalism are presented as opposites, at least in Switzerland and just before elections. I think this antithesis has become historical, to put it guardedly.

B. Yes, at election time and when party leaders speak. So there are in fact no longer any genuine or clear alternatives. No great and basic ideas seem to be in conflict any more. I am always at a loss as to which party to vote for, if any.

I. Would you say that being liberal has nothing or not very much to do with political liberalism but that it is more a human attitude which cuts across all parties?

B. Yes, I could accept that if we are to use the term. But I do not set much store by the word. If it is to be used at all I would prefer that it be used, as in our discussion, for a basic style, a human posture. What is called and calls itself liberal today, as here in Basel, could just as well . . .

I. . . . be called conservative?

B. I am glad you said it and not I. We know whom we have in mind and what paper, don't we? . . . But let them go their way in peace.

I. Well, I think that with this partial clarification of the word "liberal" we have rounded off our talk, and I want to thank you for your part in it.

B. Partial. Yes indeed, partial! For there are many other things about our theme that especially now remain to be noted and explained. But if you are satisfied with the part, then I am satisfied too.

RADIO SERMONS CATHOLIC AND EVANGELICAL

SOMEWHAT IMMOBILIZED BY PHYSICAL WEAKNESS, I have for a long time made a practice of listening on Sunday mornings to two sermons on the Swiss radio, a Roman Catholic and then an Evangelical Reformed. Usually, to emphasize their ecclesiastical and liturgical character, these sermons are accompanied by bells and choral singing, and sometimes by extracts from congregational worship. On both sides certain church authorities obviously control the choice of preachers. Thus within limits what may be heard can be taken as representative of Sunday and festal preaching both here and possibly elsewhere. I should like to offer some thoughts and impressions of my own about it.

Looking back on what I have heard I want to say first that I have lost a good deal of the anxiety, foreboding, and skepticism that I might have had regarding the public activity of the pastors of both confessions. Very little religious prattle or solemn droning has come to my ears. Serious work has stood behind all these sermons, although naturally with varying degrees of success. Among the Reformed some have been marked by prophetic power while among the Roman Catholic a series of fast sermons was characterized by mystical depth in the good sense. If I take closeness to the Bible and closeness to life as the decisive criteria of a good sermon, my impression is that with, of course, some regrettable exceptions the preaching has been good — basic, edifying, and helpful. Only in a few cases have I turned off the set in disillusionment or annoyance. In comparison with the past I may even state, with all due reservations, that preaching is on the whole better now than it was. This is palpable on the Roman Catholic side. For other reasons it is so on the Reformed side too. And I am comparing it with what I myself and my theological friends did some fifty years ago at the time of the celebrated beginnings of the dialectical theology.

A question that needs to be put to those of the Reformed persuasion is whether they are really as free and as much "reformers" as those of the good old days. Have I accidentally missed a series of sermons of that type? Where are the authentic successors of the older generation in this regard? In none or almost none of the sermons I have heard do I remember noting anything of the demythologizing and existentializing of the New Testament characteristic of that school. Mention might be made of the sermon of a Dominican early last year in Lucerne — on the ambivalent theme: "Did Jesus Die in Vain?" — but this simply serves as a reminder that the school did in its way flourish in Switzerland too, even in Roman Catholic Switzerland. But I only read this sermon in a local paper and did not hear it.

More important is the following general observation. What I have heard has been ecumenical preaching, even when the term has not been used. I mean that there has not been any confessional debate, obviously not because of some tacit or express radio agreement, but because neither side has seemed to feel any serious need for it. In spite of Chapter VIII of the Church Constitution of Vatican II, I have heard on the Roman Catholic side no extolling of the Mother of God, only muted references to the authority of the Petrine office, and no direct stress at all on the meritoriousness of good works. And on the Reformed side there have been no allusions to the power and craft of the devil resident in Rome and no insistence on "Here I stand; I can do no other." Obviously some things have been said on both sides out of respect for the fathers, but not in active attack or defense. Again, not all Roman Catholics like the Reformed style of preaching, nor do all the Reformed like the Roman Catholic style. But in what is said on either side the element of dissent is, for those who have ears to hear, much less significant than the material consensus, that is, an increasing concentration on the gospel. I heard a Roman Catholic sermon for a day of prayer which had as its setting Luther's hymn: "In deepest need I cry to thee." This is now in the Roman Catholic hymnbook, and if an important verse is left out there it was in fact sung at that particular service. In the main the serious and final focus on both sides is now on Jesus Christ. We should all be glad about this, and as for the devil, we should look for him only where this is weakly set forth rather than in the opposite confession. A reunion of churches is, in my view, still far off. But again I cannot deny that in the sermons I have heard I have seen the churches somehow on the way to this distant, or even very distant, goal. Precisely in order that this may be evident to everyone I think the practice of letting both churches have their say every Sunday should be continued. In this regard it would seem better to me if the customary playing of ostensibly or authentically serious music did not break the sequence by coming between the sermons but instead rounded off both of them and thus formed a natural transition to the rest of the Sunday morning program.

I now come to more specific matters. The strength of

Reformed preaching lies not least in its being the central point of Reformed worship. Extemporaneous or set prayers and congregational singing simply form a prelude and epilogue to it. This gives it even formally an importance, seriousness, and urgency which one misses in even the best Roman Catholic preaching. For the Reformed preacher the decisive point is to be found in his preparation for what will take place at the desk or in the pulpit on Sunday. But wait a moment! In all seriousness one might ask whether this strength of ours is not also our weakness, whether the center of worship would not be better if it had the form of an ellipse with two foci instead of a circle with only one middle point. Supposing that occasionally, or perhaps all the time, the poor man up front there has, for different reasons, nothing worthwhile to say. Even if he does, do we not expect in our services, by no means arbitrarily, that some concrete act of worship will follow which cannot be replaced by prayer, or singing, or a collection taken perhaps only on departure? In the Bible Constitution of Vatican II, even if in dubious imagery, we read that there are two tables to which the congregation is called on Sunday: the table of the Word of God which is proclaimed to it and the table of the work of God which is celebrated in the eucharist. Roman Catholic preachers, often to their disadvantage, take things more easily than ours, and their congregations with them. But please! the twofold focus in worship — preaching and the Lord's supper — was Calvin's own intention, although Geneva rejected it under pressure from Berne. Why is not the Lord's supper administered among us every Sunday in every church in the presence of the whole congregation? Even if the length of the sermons had to be cut and also the unsuitably intrusive organ music! The relaxing of preacher and congregation, of minister and those to whom he ministers, is surely legitimate. Sometimes baptism — the baptism of a responsible adult, not an infant! — might also form a good beginning so long as it is not unnecessarily wordy. In this way would we not be more comprehensively the church of the Word — of the Word which was not just talk but was made flesh?

I have called closeness to the Bible the first criterion of a good sermon. One notes that on the whole the Reformed have in this respect an older tradition and more practice, although even we have often dealt with a topic on the pretext of a verse or passage from scripture. Among Roman Catholics most sermons are expressly on subjects. This was unmistakably so in the Bultmannian address by the Lucerne Dominican and also in the sermon for a day of prayer whose content was so excellent. On another occasion, I heard a preacher say at the outset, without even announcing a text, that he was going to speak on "Psychology and Pastoral Care." In general one might also say that even the most progressive Roman Catholics preach a little more law and detailed morality than corresponds to the guidance of the Holy Spirit. But only too often this is true of our own preachers as well. And it is undeniable that the Roman Catholics are on the point of catching up in this matter of closeness to the Bible. One is touched sometimes by the zeal with which their preachers as well as ours, instead of moving briskly from text to matter, can waste the first minutes, which are so important, in imparting the familiar wisdom of historical criticism. But surely holy scripture, when its dignity is officially recognized and stressed as it is today, can also assert in Roman Catholic preaching its superiority to all the dogmatic, moral, and exegetical talk which clusters around it. To be sure, there is still too much of the thinking from below upwards which radically perverts proclamation — Thomistic among older Roman Catholics, Cartesian among many of the Reformed, and a strange mixture of the two among modern Roman Catholics. But supposing one day Roman Catholics break free from this more sharply than do the Reformed? There is already a marked development in this direction in the Roman Catholic church. How will it be then with our scripture principle?

Finally, I have described closeness to life as the second criterion of a good sermon. Now I have undoubtedly heard some Reformed sermons that are definitely remote from life. But I have found this to be a fairly general weakness of Roman Catholic preachers and one which for the moment is not being remedied. What they know of human life as it is, and as preaching must speak to it precisely when it is close to the Bible, they know only from books and the confessional and deep reflection but not — and we have to grasp the nettle here — from inside, from their own experience, at that very point where precisely in its humanity it is for good or ill most human. They can address their people very well on such matters as work and pay, politics and art, and so forth, but not authentically or effectively on the sphere where all else has either secretly or openly its nerve and center — human life in love, marriage, and family — for in this whole field they can speak only as those who take part from outside. This is because in their own lives there are no wives to be present with them day and night — perhaps with a larger or smaller brood of children — and to talk and act with them and possibly to have dealings with the congregation too. Now it is not my intention to sing the familiar song in praise of the evangelical parsonage. Nor am I in the least questioning the possibility of a freely chosen, charismatically grounded celibacy on the basis of which a Roman Catholic preacher might sometimes perhaps be able to see and discuss human life even more profoundly than many of his separated brethren, on whom is usually laid the burden of also pleasing their wives. The great example of a powerfully exercised freedom for celibacy is before us all. But the important question, which is being debated afresh in Roman Catholic circles today, is whether it was and is salutary for the church that a general rule should be made out of this particular freedom. Before closing, however, I should take a look at our Reformed preachers too. Normally the Reformed preacher is a man who knows what it means to fall in love and to be engaged and married, but obviously this is not in any way a guarantee that his sermons will really be good in the sense of being close to life. Not in the least! In practice his knowledge might even work to his disadvantage. A little more reflection on what Paul, not Peter, said about that charism might be good for evangelical preaching in our own time too.

What I have said here touches on very big problems in the ecumenical life of the churches alongside one another and together, of their distinctive dogmatics and ethics, of their pastoral theology and practice. But it could only touch on them. Therefore, using the refrain of a very secular song of Mozart, and in relation to the totality of my remarks and also the details, "I will say no more."

Starting Out, Turning Round, Confessing

DEAR CATHOLIC AND REFORMED FELLOW-CHRISTIANS: In this hour I want to talk to you about starting out, turning round, and confessing in the church. Of course there is much starting out, turning round, and confessing, or talk of it, in the world as well. The church is in the world and the world is also in the church. Thus we should never ignore or despise what goes on in the world or is at least discussed in it. If we are not to overvalue it, we are also not to undervalue it. Nevertheless, I am certain that starting out, turning round, and confessing — that of Christians — will serve us best and bring us into the deepest solidarity with what is called the world if we concern ourselves energetically with starting out, turning round, and confessing in the church.

The three concepts mentioned are not marks or essential features or structures of the church. From three different if related angles they are the one movement in which the church finds itself. There are all kinds of movements in the church. There always have been. There can and should be today. But these movements are important and good only if they derive from the one movement of the church and serve this movement. Let us speak today of the one movement of the church's starting out, turning round, and confessing by which all individual movements, if they are important and good, are determined and limited.

This one movement of the church takes place. It does not happen for the first time today. In many ages it took place in an underground way, perceived only by the few. Even today it still takes place for the most part in this underground way. In its essence it is noticed by relatively few. Nevertheless, it is taking place today much more perceptibly than in earlier times, and the number of those who perceive it in its essence is greater.

The distinctive mark of this one movement of the church, of its starting out, turning round, and confessing, consists today in the fact that in the contemporary church it is taking place in many, although not all confessions. Our particular interest here and now is that it is taking place or is visible today in the Roman Catholic, or, as I would prefer to say, the Petrine Catholic and the Evangelical Catholic confessions — for we are Catholic too. For the moment it is surprisingly more visible and even spectacular in the Petrine than in the Evangelical confession. But however that may be, there is this one movement of the one church, in our case of the two confessions. We shall have occasion at any rate to focus our attention on both of them together.

But let us get down to business.

The movement of the church is in the first instance a powerful starting out. (I should like to say something specific about the word "powerful" at the end of this address.) Starting out takes place when something already there has grown old and must be left behind, when the night is past, when something new replaces it and a new day dawns. When this is true, and is seen to be true, starting out takes place. Ancient, medieval, modern, and present-day church history is continually an open or hidden history of such starting out, sometimes greater it would seem and sometimes smaller, sometimes successful and sometimes unsuccessful. The model of all starting out — a model which can never shed enough light or be studied enough — is the exodus of Israel out of Egypt for the promised land.

Starting out takes place in a crisis. A resolute farewell is then said to what is familiar, what is close at hand, what has its own advantages, as in the form of the well-known fleshpots of Egypt. And there is a resolute turning instead to what is distant, to what is affirmed in hope, to what has disadvantages, to what is still largely unknown in its glorious form. When the church sets out, it has made a choice, a decision. It refuses to be homesick for what it leaves behind. It hails and loves already what is before it. It is still here and yet no longer here. It is not yet there but there already. It has a long journey ahead of it — battles too, and suffering, and hunger and thirst. Unmistakably it sighs. Yet unmistakably, too, it rejoices. It thinks and speaks and acts accordingly. The starting out of the church takes place in this crisis. It is that of the people of God which is still in bondage and yet already freed.

But let us look a little more closely. The true and authentic starting out of the church is first and supremely an acceptance of the future and only then and for that reason a denial of the past. Mere weariness or criticism or distaste or scorn or protest in relation to what has been thus far, to what would now be called the establishment, has nothing whatever to do with the church's great movement of starting out. When Moses killed and buried that wicked man, that was not by a long way Israel's liberation from imprisonment. In both confessions today we often hear a justifiable but empty negation — empty because it is not filled with affirmation of the better future. An empty negation will always have a more or less disagreeable and melancholy sound. When the church genuinely negates what has been thus far, it will be a clear negation, but one that is also friendly and cheerful.

It follows, then, that the church's true and authentic starting out takes place only when it sees the new as promise and therefore as future, as clear and definite promise and future. Some years ago a young man in a gathering of clergy startled me by saying, "Professor, you have made history but you have now become history. We young folk are setting out for new shores." I replied, "That is good. I am glad to hear it. Tell me something about these new shores." Unfortunately he had nothing to tell. The exodus from Egypt began when Moses came down from the mount of God and away from the burning bush, where he had heard God's Word, and was thus able to tell the people and Pharaoh something about where they were going. In the church today there are many likable young people, including young pastors and priests, who tell us very loudly that almost everything must be changed. If only God would tell them, or if they would let God tell them, and if they would then tell others, what is to replace the present set-up, then and only then their activity would have something authentically and credibly to do with the starting out of the church.

Just a final remark on the first point. The true and authentic starting out of the church will have to take place in an orderly way. Naturally until the caravan is reorganized and the march has begun, there will be some confusion. The more conservative and more progressive groups in the church will not be in total agreement as to how things should be done. The former will sadly demand that as much as possible of the old should be taken along. The latter in an onrush of joy will tell them that everything must be different. There will also be Christian hippies whose mouths the ecclesiastical police will find it very hard to shut, not to speak of dropouts and the like. But these transitional phenomena must not be allowed to degenerate into permanent confusion. The departure of the church has to be a more or less disciplined event in which there are no winners and no losers. The charism of *gyberneseos*, the gift of government or leadership, comes into its own here. In the Old Testament story of the exodus Moses was a classical bearer of this gift, and at the time of the reformation so, too, was Calvin, as distinct from Luther and Zwingli. It is not for nothing that in our time a Roman Catholic historian [has devoted] a fine volume to Calvin as seen from this angle. The only pity is that on the Petrine Catholic side there was no likeminded Aaron who had to be taken with equal seriousness. If there had been, perhaps the church could have started out then with comprehensive instead of divided ranks.

The church has its origin in the command of Jesus Christ. It looks and moves toward his new and glorious coming. This is why its starting out, indeed, its whole movement, is such a positive, goal-oriented, and orderly event.

Secondly, the movement of the church is a powerful turning round. The word "Forward" and the word "Back" are not self-contradictory in the church. Instead they denote the one movement.

In the church the word "conversion" means turning in one's tracks and then starting off toward the new thing, the goal that is ahead. It is a turning back toward what has already happened originally because only in movement toward this oldest thing of all can there be a right starting out for what is new and future. One of the basic notes of the Old Testament sounds out unmistakably here: "For ask now of the days that are past . . . Did any people ever hear the voice of God speaking out of the midst of the fire, as you have heard. . . ? Has God ever attempted to go and take a nation from the midst of another nation . . . according to all that the Lord your God did for you in Egypt before your eyes?" (Dt. 4:32f.); or again: "Stand by the roads and look, and ask for the ancient paths, what the way of salvation is; and walk in it, and find rest for your souls" (Jer. 6:16).

One must consider carefully, however, what is meant by this common backward movement of the church to see if it is true and authentic turning round.

True and authentic turning round will always see the old to which it turns back as the new for which it is on the point of starting out. By the fact that it is the new, the old here is distinguished from the old things that must be left behind if the church is to start out. For Evangelical Christians that means that it will not be identical with the liberal theology and piety of the nineteenth century from which we have come, nor even, and this has been true since 1517, with the reformation of the sixteenth century and its offshoots in the seventeenth and eighteenth centuries. Again, and this applies to you, dear Petrine fellow-Christians, it will not be identical with the world of Trent and Vatican I and what for the last one hundred and fifty years has been rather romantically called the philosophy and theology of the former days, namely, medieval scholasticism, the fathers, and the first Christian centuries. Listening to the past might be a beautiful idea, but it is not a churchly one either among you or us. On both sides the old to which the church turns back in true and authentic conversion is valid only as in and with and under it there takes place the new for which the church is starting out. Mark you, what we have been saying applies even to the so-called primitive Christianity whose contours as something old may be seen by us in the New Testament. The church does not turn back to primitive Christianity but to the new which is, of course, primarily, directly, and normatively attested for all times in its first records. Paul did not proclaim himself but the crucified and risen Jesus Christ. So, too, in their own ways did Peter and John and also the Evangelists. He, Jesus Christ, is the old and is also new. He it is who comes [to the church] and to whom the church goes, but goes to him as him who was. It is to him that it turns in its conversion.

But now we must underline the other side too. Seeing that the starting out of the church is a starting out to its origin, the turning round of the church that takes place in and with it is always an act of respect and gratitude in relation to the old which for its part has proceeded in some sense from this origin: not because it is old, not in relation to everything that is old, but in relation to much of the old in which the new, closely viewed, already intimates itself, and in which, carefully handled, the new may also be detected. Israel had before it the patriarchs: Abraham, who in faith left his country and friends for the land that God would show him and did show him; then Isaac and Jacob and the fathers of the tribal league which after a time was brought into the land. And this land that was promised and given to Israel was itself, according to the tradition, none other than that in which the patriarchs as guests had lived and sinned and suffered and set up altars here and there to the Lord. In the church that is in the process of turning round the saying is true that "God is not the God of the dead but of the living." "All live to him," from the apostles to the earlier and later fathers. They have not only the right [but also the relevance] to be heard today, not uncritically, not in automatic subjection, but still attentively. The church would not be the church in conversion if, proud and content with [?] its sense of the present hour, it would not listen to them, or would do so only occasionally, loosely, and carelessly, or if it were to rob what it has to learn from them of all its effect by [accepting] what they want to say to it. . . .

EPILOGUE

By Eberhard Busch

The pieces of Karl Barth which have been collected here are no more than small contributions in which, according to the powers and possibilities still available to him in old age, he tried to participate a little, as he would say, in present-day theology. What they have in common is first that they were in fact the last utterances that he prepared for publication. All of them were written after his severe crisis of health in August, 1968, when it had also become clear to him that he could not continue that winter the colloquies which he had conducted at Basel University the four preceding semesters. Again, they all arose in the beautiful autumn fullness which was granted to his life in the remaining weeks after that sickness.

The first of the essays is his brief answer to the question which a Paris newspaper put to him regarding his testimony who and what Jesus Christ was for him. It was published in November, 1968, in *La Table Ronde*, No. 250, 14f. The next two pieces are interviews on the German Swiss radio. Some editing has been done here. The first is a talk in Basel dialect (November 17, 1968) with Roswitha Schmalenbach on the popular series "Music for a Guest," in which the conversation is interrupted from time to time by selected records. The German version has been prepared by Franziska Zellweger-Barth. The second interview, not broadcast until April 7, 1969, consists of a talk with Alfred Blatter in connection with a questionnaire on the general subject of liberalism. The fourth essay, also composed for and delivered on the radio, presents some thoughts of Barth as a regular listener in his old age to radio sermons. He found these especially interesting because they gave him the very welcome ecumenical opportunity of hearing successively each Sunday a Roman Catholic and a Reformed sermon. (On December 8 he was especially glad to hear a Roman Catholic sermon on the subject of Mary's conception!)

The final piece printed here is the very last of all his works. At the beginning of December a Roman Catholic professor named J. Feiner asked Barth if on the occasion of the ecumenical week of prayer (January 18, 1969) he would deliver an address to a meeting of Roman Catholic and Reformed Christians in the Paulusakademie in Zurich. In discharging this task Barth chose on his own a theme that he thought would be pertinent to both groups of hearers and the dominant tendencies on both sides. To make it sound less legal and more of an invitation and an event, he intentionally decided to put the title in the verbal nouns: "Starting Out, Turning Round, Confessing." Up to the evening of December 9 he worked diligently and faithfully on the manuscript for this address, pausing only to read the books of Gertrud Lendorff on the colorful background of old Basel. He broke off the text in the middle of a sentence, hoping to complete the half-finished address the following day. But he did not live through to the morning. In the middle of the night he died suddenly but peacefully.

If the final essay is to be understood the following points should be noted. As indicated, the text is incomplete. It is so, however, in two senses. For one thing the first half, although written down, can be regarded only as a first draft. Given the way Barth composed his works, one can be sure that when dictating and revising it he would not only have improved the style but also made more or less extensive corrections and amplifications. (One or two words have been proposed in the present version where Barth left gaps.) But, then again, the present text is incomplete in the sense that the last and shorter part was never written at all. The work must therefore be read as a fragment which breaks off in the middle. To give some help in reading it, we may observe that the unfinished sentence would probably have continued something like this: ". . . by accepting what they want to say to it, perhaps with much reverence, but only as a statement of the insights of their own day." As regards the final section, which Barth never worked out, we may be glad that he had for his main headings a rough outline which can give us some idea at least of what he would have said. For the last part of the address it runs as follows:

Confessing	Yes and Amen	Mission
	Mystery	Nature?
	Conscience?	The World
Conclusion	To what Extent already Event?	
	Body and Blood	Epiphany
	I am — You are	
	Taking with Joyful Seriousness	

For those who find this outline somewhat cryptic, it might perhaps be explained as follows. Confessing takes place correctly only as confession of him in whom all the promises of God are Yes and Amen (2 Cor. 1:10). Hence, it is not, as among many supporters and op-

ponents of the papal encyclical *Humani generis,* the
confession of various insights of nature and conscience.
For in these, as Barth wrote in a letter just before, we
have Yes and No and no Amen. At the same time this
confessing cannot be a private matter but must be
public thinking, speaking, and acting in and for the
world. It is not to be done in self-assertion but in
the mission which is essential to the church as such —
not in self-assertion, because what is confessed in
this confessing remains a mystery for Christians
themselves. The starting out, turning round, and confessing of the church is already an event in the power
of the epiphany of Jesus Christ. This epiphany is not
made possible by the one and threefold movement. On
the contrary, it itself makes the movement possible,
because in manifesting what he is it also manifests what
we already are. Thus the whole movement arises for us,
and takes place correctly, only when we take with joyful seriousness what we are in what he is. The characteristic and instructive form of this taking with joyful
seriousness, however, is an act which is to be understood and celebrated afresh (each Sunday). This is the
act of eucharist for the once-for-all giving and ef-
ficacious gift of the body and blood of Jesus Christ.

This account is, of course, only an explanation and
not a development of the outline. It does not in any
sense convey the inimitable originality of Barth in
working out his themes. One can see this plainly by
looking at the outline for the first two sections and
comparing it with the development in the address
itself.

Introduction	Starting Out (etc.) of the Church
	of the one Church
	Movement Yet also Event

Starting Out	Crisis, Departure —
	New Shores Tumult?
	But Passover Hippies?
	And Promise
	(On a separate sheet)
	Not just Negation
	But Goal — Position!
	Alternative!
	Promise
	Under Leadership
	Orderly
	From X (Christ) and to X
Turning Round	Israel Aggiornamento?
	Scripture Good old Days
	(On a separate sheet)
	New-Old Time
	Aggiornamento-
	Accommodation?
	Is.51:1; Dt.4:32; Jer.6:16
	Listening to the Past?
	Early Theology
	Abraham, Isaac . . .
	Renaissance
	Historicism?

It must be repeated that in Barth's own view the five pieces assembled here were no more than little statements, differing greatly in content and importance, and corresponding to the resources at his disposal with advancing age. It is in a sense only accidentally that they are the final testimonies of his intellectual and theological endeavor. He did not view them as parts of a theological testament. In his old age, astonished at having achieved it, he preserved a quiet but lively awareness that things might be different at nightfall from what they were in early morning. But he never had any serious thought of composing a theological testament. If readers want this, they should faithfully read or read again the volumes of the *Church Dogmatics*. And they should read with particular attention the fragment of the *Church Dogmatics* IV, 4 on baptism. Whether standing to the theological right or left or in the center, they will certainly find there to their satisfaction Barth's theological testament.

Yet, obviously, in the present writings we have much more than an accident. It is no accident that at the end of Barth's life the confession of Jesus Christ comes out so centrally and dominantly. It is no accident that in his final utterances participation in ecumenical discussion holds so large a place. It is no accident that his last express task was to invite positive and liberal Christians, both Evangelical and Roman Catholic, to the one necessary movement of starting out, turning round, and confessing. It is no accident that the pen was finally taken from his fingers when he was reminding us that in trust in the God who is the God of the living and not the dead we should also listen to the fathers who have gone before us in the faith. In fact it can and should and will be certain that his accidentally final testimonies will after his death speak to us in a special way as a final legacy. In fact we can and should already regard it as an important and noteworthy legacy that even with increasing evidence of his temporal limits he simply stuck to his task and alertly labored on literally to the very end. And in fact we should indeed view it as his costly and instructive legacy that precisely at the last he talked as he did and could, so peacefully and cheerfully, but also so freely and relevantly, so concretely and responsibly, and also so edifyingly and encouragingly.

If we have listened to what he said in these final testimonies, and how he said it, only fools can bewail his death as unexpectedly sudden and premature; instead we should think of him with gratitude and consolation: *Lux aeterna lucet ei perpetua.* If we have really listened to what he said in these final testimonies, and how he said it, we shall forbid any decorating of the grave of this prophet (Mt. 23:29). Instead we shall let ourselves be invited and summoned joyfully and humbly, prayerfully and confidently, to start out, turn round, and confess. And we shall undoubtedly find it well advised, and by no means unprofitable, to listen to this father of the church too, and by him to be properly taught concerning the basis, goal, and meaning of the new starting out, turning round, and confessing which we all need.

Printed in Great Britain
by Amazon.co.uk, Ltd.,
Marston Gate.